Rude Rhymes

Rude Rhymes

Mother Goose Goes Behind the Bike Sheds

Collected by
Michael Rosen

Cartoons by Riana Duncan

ANDRE DEUTSCH

First published in 1989 by
André Deutsch Limited
105–106 Great Russell Street, London WC1B 3LJ

ISBN 0 233 98467 4

Typeset by AKM Associates (UK) Ltd,
Ajmal House, Hayes Road, Southall, London
Printed and bound in Great Britain by
WBC Ltd, Bristol & Maesteg

Foreword

Ah childhood! Time of blissful ignorance and innocence. Time when we adults must lower our voices when talking of sex; time when we should maintain a decent silence about what goes on behind the toilet-door.

But hang on! What happens if you ask children what rhymes and jokes they know? Or even more interesting, what happens if you ask adults what rhymes and jokes they remember from their childhood? A flood of verses are sung or chanted at you. Various collections of these have been published, but it wasn't the whole picture and people asked: 'Where are all those *rude* rhymes we told each other when we were young? Aren't children telling them anymore?' Well, they are – but the rude ones were left out because they were too rude for the children!

Now, at long last, in pocket format, ideal for train journey, winter evening or loo reading, come the missing rhymes. They have all been collected orally either from children who guessed I was too depraved to deprave or from adults remembering their childhood, who agreed I was depraved but discovered that they were too. If you're after being amazed and amused start at the beginning – but remember – not in front of the children, they may want to know why you're laughing.

If you know any more, why not contribute to Volume II? Send your rhymes to Michael Rosen, c/o André Deutsch, 105, Great Russell Street, London WC1B 3LJ. Please give details of from whom, how old (or young), and where. Your reward will be a free copy and, if you're willing to own up to it, an acknowledgement.

Tune: Colonel Bogey

Hitler has only got one ball.
The other is in the county hall.
His mother, the dirty bugger,
Cut it off, when he was small.

boy, 11
London

SALVATION ARMY

'Sister Anna will carry the banner!'
'But I carried it last week!'
'You'll carry it every bloody week!'
'But I'm in the family way!'
'You're in every bugger's way!'

man, 60
Middlesex

Tune: Villikins and Dinah

As Rachel was walking in the garden one day,
'Sei geschwind, sei geschwind', her mother did say.
'Go and put on your best shabbes clothes
Chaim schmerel is waiting with the big grobbe nose.

'sei geschwind' = *be quick*
'shabbes' = *sabbath*
'Chaim' is a name (James)
'schmerel' = *fool*
'grobbe' = *horrible, gross*

man, 68
London

Hunch Bunch, call the Judge,
Mother's having a baby.
Is it a boy?
Is it a girl?
Is it a human baby?

Wrap it up in tissue paper.
Throw it down the escalator.
First floor – drop.
Second floor – drop.
Third floor – kick the door.
Mother's not having a baby no more.

girl, 12
London

I went into a treacle shop
to buy half a pound a treacle
and who do you think I met?
Mickey Thumb.
He asked me if I'd go to the fair,
and I thought a bit
and I thought a bit
and I said I didn't mind.
And it were a fair.

So I come home
and took me bonnet off
and a knock came at the door
and who do you think that was?
Mickey Thumb's uncle
to say that he were ill
and would I go and visit him.
So I thought a bit
and I thought a bit
and I said I didn't mind.
And he were ill.

I came in
took me bonnet off
and a knock came at the door
and who do you think that was?
Mickey Thumb's father
to say that he were dead
and would I go to the funeral.
So I thought a bit
and I thought a bit
and I said I didn't mind.
And it were a funeral.

Some laughed over his grave
Some cried over his grave
but I spat over his grave
in 'membrance of Mickey Thumb.

girl, 12, London
learnt from mother (Manchester)

Sung

Rudolph the red-nosed reindeer
had a very shiny cock
and if you ever touched it
you'd get an electric shock.

girl, 10
London

Sung

I don't care if it snows or freezes,
I am Jesus' little lamb.
I am safe in the arms of Jesus
Yes, by Jesus Christ, I am.

man, 68
London

Fatty and Skinny went up in a rocket,
Fatty came down with shit in his pocket.

Fatty and Skinny in bed,
Fatty rolled over and Skinny was dead.

boy, 7
London

The angle of the dangle
is proportional to the sag of the bag
as long as the heat of the meat
remains constant.

man, 44
Hertfordshire

Every little bean
must be heard
as well as seen.

man, 69
London

In days of old
when knights were bold
and people were contented,
they wiped their arse
on a piece of glass
and drove themselves demented.

man, 70
London

Rice an' peas an' ackee,
stick it up your battee,
mix it roun' with gravy,
an' feed it to the bald head baby.

girl, 12
London

The boy stood on the burning deck
eating a tuppeny Walls,
a bit dropped down his trouser leg
and paralysed his balls.

The boy stood on the burning deck
playing a game of cricket,
the ball flew down his trouser leg
and hit his middle wicket.

man, 42
Middlesex

DIRTY BOOKS

Rusty Bedsprings
by I.P. Knightly

Twenty Years in the Saddle
by Major Bumsore

Dirty Walls
by Hoo Flung Dung

1 girl, 13, London
2, 3 man, 42
London

Ask your mother for fifty cents
to see the lion jump the fence.
He jumped so high
he touched the sky
and didn't come back
till the 4th of July.

Ask your mother for fifty more
to see the lion swim ashore.
He swam so fast
he cut his arse
on a piece of
looking glass.

man, 68
London

Ta-ra-ra Boom-de-ay!
My knickers flew away,
I found them on a motorway.

girl, 12
London

Little Miss Muffet sat on a tuffet
her knickers all tattered and torn.
It wasn't the spider that sat down beside 'er;
It was Little Boy Blue with the horn.

girl, 14
London

Sung

Passengers will please refrain
from urinating while the train
is standing in the station
or a s-i-i-i-iding.

woman, 65
London

These two tramps were walking along the road
when they came to a pile of dog shit.
They looked at it
and one said,
It looks like it.
The other said,
It feels like it.
Then one said,
It tastes like it.
Then they stepped over it and said,
Lucky we didn't tread in it.

man, 42
Middlesex

On the door of 'The Wee Room'

We aim to please,
You aim, too, please.

girl, 13
London

Down in the lavatory
ten foot deep,
there lies a sausage
fast asleep.
Do not stir him
he's at rest.
Beecham's pills
have done their best.

man, 42
Middlesex

Mary had a little lamb
she thought it very silly,
she threw it up into the air
and caught it by its willy
was a bull-dog sitting on the grass,
along came a bumble-bee
and stung him on the
ask no questions,
tell no lies,
I never seen a copper
doing up his flies
are a nuisance,
bees are worse.
That's the end
of my silly verse.

girl, 13
London

My big mum
has a very big bum
and a very big bum has she.
She sits in the dark
in the middle of the park
scratching her bum like me.

boy, 11
London

Sung

Everybody's doing it, doing it, doing it,
Picking their nose and chewing it, chewing it.

man, 42
Middlesex

The higher up the mountain
the sweeter grows the grass,
the higher up the donkey climbs
the more it shows its face.

man, 68
London

My name's Ben
and I live in a tree,
sell condoms
for 25p.
I would sell them
for a half a bob,
but that all depends
on the size of your knob.

boy, 11
London

Little winkles in their shells,
I think it is a sin,
to pick the little buggers out
and eat them off a pin.

woman, 25
London

Big Ben
strikes ten
does a fart
now and then.

boy, 7
London

Tune: The Snowman (as in film)

We're walking through the air,
I've lost my underwear
I'm going to Mothercare
to buy
another pair
to wear . . .

boy, 8
London

Sung

Miss Nancy have a baby.
She call it Tiny Tim.
She put it in the bath tub
to see if it can swim.
It dive to the bottom
it dive to the top.
Miss Nancy get excited
and grab him by his
i-tiddly-i-tee
i-tiddly-i-tee . . .

boy, 9
London

Mary had a little lamb
and a little duck,
she put them on the mantlepiece
to see if they would fall off.

man, 42
Middlesex

Tune: Sam Hall

His name was Knobbly Hall, Knobbly Hall;
His name was Knobbly Hall, Knobbly Hall;
His name was Knobbly Hall
and he only had one ball.
His name was Knobbly Hall, Knobbly Hall.

He went to rob a bank, rob a bank;
He went to rob a bank, rob a bank;
He went to rob a bank
on the way he had a wank.
He went to rob a bank, rob a bank.

The policeman caught him quick, caught him quick;
The policeman caught him quick, caught him quick;
The policeman caught him quick
and hung him by his dick.
The policeman caught him quick, caught him quick.

The judge's name was Hunt, his name was Hunt;
The judge's name was Hunt, his name was Hunt;
The judge's name was Hunt
he was a silly cunt.
The judge's name was Hunt, his name was Hunt.

They hung poor Knobbly Hall, Knobbly Hall;
They hung poor Knobbly Hall, Knobbly Hall;
They hung poor Knobbly Hall
by his last remaining ball.
They hung poor Knobbly Hall, Knobbly Hall.

They buried him in a pit, in a pit;
They buried him in a pit, in a pit;
They buried him in a pit
that pit was full of shit.
They buried him in a pit, in a pit.

girl, 10,
London

Um Chukka Willy
of Coconut Grove
was a mean motherfucker
you could tell by his clothes.
Black leather jacket
and hairy arse,
between his balls was a patch of grass,
led a hundred women
through a hole in the wall,
swore to the devil
he'd fuck'em all.
At ninety nine
he had to stop,
the friction on his balls
was about to pop.
Went to the doctor
and the doctor said,
'Um Chukka Willy
your balls are dead.'

boy, 11
London

Tune: Signature tune for 'Rainbow'

Flying up above streets and houses
Bungle's flying high,
opens up his hairy arse
and shits in Jeffrey's eye.

boy, 7
London

I'm not dumb,
I'm not silly,
I hang on
to daddy's willy.

boy, 11
London

Say 'Polish it in the corner' very quickly over and over
   again.

man, 42
Middlesex

Tune: Ten Green Bottles

Ten black widows hanging on a wall.
Ten black widows hanging on a wall,
and if one black widow
should accidentally fall,
she will climb up his trousers
and paralyse his balls.

boy, 8
London

'RAINBOW'

In the jungle
Zippy and Bungle
having lots of fun;
Zippy got silly
and pulled out his willy
and shoved it up Bungle's bum.

boys, 12
London

Tune: Mademoiselle from Armentières

There was an old lady of ninety two – parlez-vous.
There was an old lady of ninety two – parlez-vous.
There was an old lady of ninety two,
she done a fart but missed the loo,
inky pinky parlez-vous.

The fart went rolling down the street – parlez-vous.
The fart went rolling down the street – parlez-vous.
The fart went rolling down the street,
knocked a copper off his feet,
inky pinky parlez-vous.

The copper got out his rusty pistol – parlez-vous.
The copper got out his rusty pistol – parlez-vous.
The copper got out his rusty pistol,
he shot the fart from here to Bristol,
inky pinky parlez-vous.

Bristol City were playing at home – parlez-vous.
Bristol City were playing at home – parlez-vous.
Bristol City were playing at home,
they kicked the fart from here to Rome,
inky pinky parlez–vous.

Julius Caesar was drinking some gin – parlez-vous.
Julius Caesar was drinking some gin – parlez-vous.
Julius Caesar was drinking some gin,
he opened his mouth and the fart popped in,
inky pinky parlez–vous.

The fart went rolling down his spine – parlez-vous.
The fart went rolling down his spine – parlez-vous.
The fart went rolling down his spine,
banged his balls and made them chime,
inky pinky parlez-vous.

Now that's the end of my little song – parlez-vous.
That's the end of my little song – parlez–vous.
That's the end of my little song,
but the fart goes rolling on,
inky pinky parlez–vous.

boy, 17
London

Old King Cole
was a merry old soul
and a merry old soul was he.
He called for a light
in the middle of the night
to go to the lavatory.
The moon shone bright
on the shit-house door;
the candle had a fit.
Old King Cole
fell down the hole
and came out covered in shit.

girl, 13
London

Down in the valley where the grass grows green,
the white cat sat on the sewing machine.
The sewing machine went so fast,
it put ten stitches in the white cat's arse.

woman, 38
Northern Ireland

'tis dogs' delight
to bark and bite
and little birds to sing,
but when the beastly fly comes round
it shits on everything.

man, 55

Mavis had a little dog
of all she loved him most.
He lifted up his little leg
and peed against the post,
but when the post began to steam
he thought it was on fire,
so he lifted up his little leg
and peed a little higher.

girl, 13
London

Hey fiddle fiddle
the cat done a piddle
all over the bathroom mat.
The little dog laughed
to see such fun
so he peed all over the cat.

Hey fiddle fiddle
the dog done a piddle
all over the kitchen floor.
The little dog laughed
to see such fun
so he done a little bit more.

girl, 13
London

Oh where is my smokey
all covered in sand?
I killed a Leeds United supporter
with an elastic band.

I went to his funeral
I went to his grave
the vicar came up to me
and asked me my name.
I answered politely
with a bicycle chain.

He took me to court for this
and the judge so did say,
'You will go to Borstal
for a year and one day.'

Me old woman fainted
me old man dropped dead,
and me poor little brother
shot the judge in the head.

There's bars on the windows
there's bars on the door
and even the piss pot
is chained to the floor.

boy, 12
London

Every little helps,
as the old man said
as he pissed in the sea.

man, 68
London

Three nudes in a fountain,
Along comes handsome Errol Flynn.
Out comes his hairy monster
Which one will he stuff it in?

Make it mine, make it mine, make it mine.

girl, 13
London

Sung

Auntie Mary had a canary
up the leg of her drawers.
When she farted
it departed
to a round of applause.

man, 22
Hertfordshire

Sung

In
the
South
of
France
where the naked ladies dance
singing:
'Milly, put your willy, next to mine . . .'

girl, 13
London

Sung

I went to a Chinese restaurant
to buy a loaf of bread, bread, bread.
They wrapped it up in a five pound note
and this is what they said, said, said:

My name is Diana Dors
I'm a movie star,
I've got cute, cute tits
and a see-through bra.
I've got the lips, lips, lips,
I've got the hips, hips, hips;
turn around
movie star -ah-ah.

girls, 7
London

The boy stood on the burning deck
his father called him lobbes
because he wouldn't wash his face
and go to schul on shabbes.

'lobbes' = lout
'schul' = synagogue
'shabbes' = sabbath

man 68
London

Jack and Jill went up the hill
to fetch a pail of water.
I don't know what they did up there
but they came down with a daughter.

Jack and Jill went up the hill
to fetch a pail of water.
I don't know what they did up there
but I know they never oughta.

boys, 12
London

Sung

My old man's a dustman
he wears a dustman's hat,
he killed two thousand Germans
so what do you think of that?

One lay here,
one lay there,
one lay round the corner.
One lay up Dusty Street
crying out for water.
Water, water, water,
water came at last,
I don't want no water
so stick it up your elbow.

boy, 12
London

Tune: Lavender's Blue

Bogwater blue, willy willy,
bogwater blue.
When I have weed, willy willy,
bogwater green.

woman, 39
Herts

Tune: John Brown's Body

She wears her silk pyjamas in the summer when it's hot,
she wears her winter woollies in the winter when it's not.
But sometimes in the springtime,
and sometimes in the fall,
she pops between the sheets
with nothing on at all.

That's the time you wanna be there,
That's the time you wanna be there,
That's the time you wanna be there,
when she pops between the sheets
with nothing on at all.

man, 68
London

Matthew Mark Luke and John
went to bed with their trousers on.
Luke woke up in the middle of the night
and said he had to do a shite.

Now a shite is a thing that must be done,
so out of the window he popped his bum.
PC Parker on his midnight beat
mistook his arse for a burglar's feet.
'Come down, you rascal,' the copper did cry.
Wallop, dollop, shit fell in his eye.

man, 68
London

Little Boy Brown
went to town
riding on a donkey;

did a fart
in the cart
and made the wheels go wonky.

boy, 8
London

I had a little poodle dog
a poodle dog was he.
He lifted up his poodle leg
and poodled over me.

girl, 12
London

Tune: William Brown (verse only)

When I was a wee wee tot,
they took me from my wee wee cot,
they put me on my wee wee pot
to see if I would wee or not.

When they found that I would not,
they took me from my wee wee pot.
They put me in my wee wee cot
where I wee wee quite a lot.

girl, 13
London

Sung: Jesus Christ Superstar

Jesus Christ, Superstar!
Come down to earth on a Yamaha.
Done a skid,
killed a kid,
and mashed his balls
on a dustbin lid.

boy, 11
London

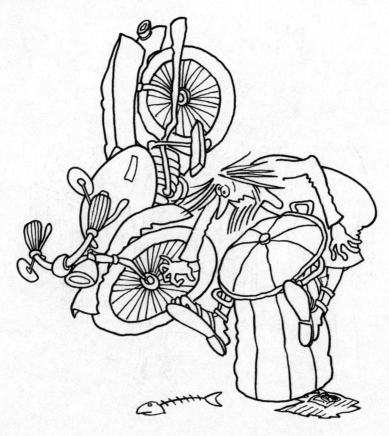

Sung

I'm Popeye the sailor man,
I live in a caravan.
There's a hole in the middle
where I do my piddle.
I'm Popeye the sailor man,
poop, poop.

I'm Popeye the sailor man,
I live in a frying pan.
Turn up the gas
burn up my ass.
I'm Popeye the sailor man,
poop, poop.

I'm Popeye the sailor man,
I live in a caravan.
When I go swimming
I kiss all the women.
I'm Popeye the sailor man,
poop, poop.

I'm Popeye the sailor man,
I live in a pot of jam.
And it's so sticky
it sticks to my dicky.
I'm Popeye the sailor man,
poop, poop.

boys, 8 and 11
London

DIRTY DEFINITIONS

The height of agony:
sliding down a razor blade
using your knob as a brake.

A cad:
someone who goes round a johnny factory
with a pin
putting holes in all the johnny bags.

Height of luxury:
fur-lined johnny
with a zip fastener

Height of impossibility:
a flea wiping an elephant's arse
with a piece of confetti.

man, 42
Middlesex

There was an old man from Guyana
who learnt how to play the piano.
His fingers slipped
and his fly buttons ripped
and out popped a hairy banana.

man, 42
Middlesex

Sung

I had the German measles,
I had them very bad,
They wrapped me in a blanket,
And put me in a van.
The van was very bumpy,
And I nearly tumbled out,
And when I got to hospital,
I heard a baby shout:
'Mama, Dadda, take me home,
From this little rusty home,
I've been here for a week or two
And Oh I want to stay with you.'
Here comes Doctor Glannister,
Sliding on a banister
Half way down he ripped his pants,
And now he's doing a cha-cha dance.

girl, 9
Northern Ireland

I love you, I love you, I love you almighty.
I wish your pyjamas were next to my nightie.
I hope you're not mistaken, I hope I haven't tricked you
I mean on the clothes line and not in the bed.

boy, 9
London

Sung

Down by the river
where nobody goes,
there's a Margaret Thatcher
picking her nose,
with a pick pick here
and a pick pick there
that's how Margaret picks her nose.

girls, 7
London

Sung

My boyfriend gave me an apple,
my boyfriend gave me a pear,
my boyfriend gave me a kiss on the lips
and threw me down the stairs.

I gave him back his apple,
I gave him back his pear,
I gave him back his kiss on the lips
and I threw him down the stairs.

He took me to the pictures,
to see a sexy film,
and when I wasn't looking
he kissed another girl.

I threw him over Italy,
I threw him over France.
I threw him over Germany
and he landed on his arse.

girls, 7
London

Is Mr Jones free?
No, but he's very reasonable.

man, 60
Middlesex

'Children children.'
'Yes mama.'
'Where were you?'
'At grandmama's.'
'What did you eat?'
'Cheese and bread.'
'Where's my share?'
'Up in the air.'
'How shall I get it?'
'Stand on a broken chair.'
'Suppose I fall? . . .'
'I don't care.'
'Who taught you manners?'
'The dog.'
'Who's the dog?'
'YOU!'

boy, 12
London, Jamaican origin

There was an old man called Denzil
whose prick was as sharp as a pencil.
It went through an actress,
three sheets and a mattress
and shattered a bedroom utensil.

man, 42
Middlesex

Sung

Honey you can't love two,
Honey you can't love two.
You can't love two
and still be true.
Honey you can't love two.
Lie down
oh boy
gee whizz.

Honey you can't love three,
Honey you can't love three.
You can't love three
and still love me,
Honey you can't love three.
Lie down
oh boy
gee whizz.

Honey you can't love four,
Honey you can't love four.
You can't love four
and still want more.
Honey you can't love four.
Lie down
oh boy
gee whizz.

Honey you can't love five,
Honey you can't love five.
You can't love five
and still be alive.
Honey you can't love five.
Lie down
oh boy
gee whizz.

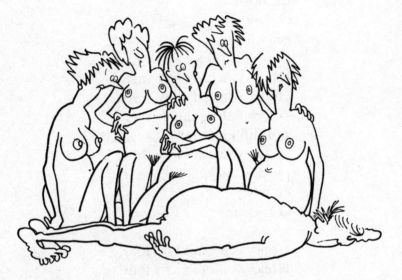

Honey you can't love six,
Honey you can't love six.
You can't love six
and play tricks.
Honey you can't love six.
Lie down
oh boy
gee whizz.

Honey you can't love seven,
Honey you can't love seven.
You can't love seven
and still go to heaven,
Honey you can't love seven.
Lie down
oh boy
gee whizz.

Honey you can't love eight,
Honey you can't love eight.
You can't love eight
and still play straight.
Honey you can't love eight.
Lie down
oh boy
gee whizz.

Honey you can't love nine,
Honey you can't love nine.
You can't love nine
and still be mine.
Honey you can't love nine.
Lie down
oh boy
gee whizz.

girl, 11
London

Chanted

One plus one,
my story's just begun
in the bedroom —
de ler-der, de ler-der
de lerdle erdle er-der.

Two plus two,
I'm telling it to you
in the bedroom —
de ler-der, de ler-der
de lerdle erdle er-der.

Three plus three,
he sat me on my knee
in the bedroom —
de ler-der, de ler-der
de lerdle erdle er-der.

Four plus four,
he got me on the floor
in the bedroom —
de ler-der, de ler-der
de lerdle erdle er-der.

Five plus five,
my legs are open wide
in the bedroom —
de ler-der, de ler-der
de lerdle erdle er-der.

Six plus six,
he's sucking at my tits
in the bedroom —
de ler-der, de ler-der
de lerdle erdle er-der.

Seven plus seven,
I think I'm up in heaven
in the bedroom —
de ler-der, de ler-der
de lerdle erdle er-der.

Eight plus eight,
the doctor's at the gate
in the bedroom —
de ler-der, de ler-der
de lerdle erdle er-der.

Nine plus nine,
the twins are doing fine
in the bedroom —
de ler-der, de ler-der
de lerdle erdle er-der.

Ten plus ten,
we're starting it again
in the bedroom —
de ler-der, de ler-der
de lerdle erdle er-der.

girl, 9
London

Tune: Teddy Bears Picnic

If you go down to the woods today
you're sure to have a surprise.
If you go down to the woods today
you'll never believe your eyes,
because mum and dad are having a screw,
Uncle Frank is having a wank
and Auntie D is having it off with grandad.

girl, 9
London

She said: 'Would you like to kiss me?'
So he kissed her.
She said: 'Would you like to undress me?'
So he undressed her.
She said: 'Take your clothes off.'
So he took his clothes off.
She said: 'Get into bed with me.'
So he got into bed with her.
She said: 'Now do the dirtiest thing you know
in the whole wide world.'
So he got out of bed
and wrote 'BUM' on the wall.

man, 42
Middlesex

Walking in the jungle,
stick in me hand,
I'm a mean motherfucker,
I'm a condom man.
Look up in the tree,
what do I see?
Another motherfucker
trying to piss on me.

Picked up a rock,
threw it at his cock.
Oh my god!
he must have got
some helluva shock.

boy, 11
London

Tune: Sam Hall

There was a man called Hunt in Waterloo,
There was a man called Hunt in Waterloo,
There was a man called Hunt
who thought he had a cunt,
but his arse was on his front
in Waterloo.

There was a man called Nest in Waterloo,
There was a man called Nest in Waterloo,
There was a man called Nest
who thought he had two breasts,
but his bum was on his chest
in Waterloo.

boy, 11
London

There's a copper round the corner
eating cherry pie.
I asked him for a skinny bit
and he poked me in the eye,
I went and told me mother,
me mother wouldn't come.
I went and got a lollipop
and stuck it up his bum.

woman, 30
Birmingham

Never kiss your lover at the garden gate,
'cos love is blind
but the neighbours ain't.

boy, 9
London

Wee Willie Winkie runs through the town
with his knickers hanging down.

boy, 11
Northern Ireland

Sung: One Man Went To Mow

One man went to mow,
went to mow a meadow;
one man went to mow,
went to mow a meadow;
one man went to mow,
went to mow a meadow;
one man and his dog, Spot,
a bottle of pop
sausage roll
pink ice-cream
change at Bank for Golders Green
Old Mother Riley and her cow
to milk it, to milk it,
she didn't know how,
she pulled its tail
instead of its tit
and all she got
was a bucketful of shit
went to mow a meadow.

man, 42
Middlesex

Tune: Stand Up Stand Up For Jesus

Sit down
sit down
for Christ's sake,
the buggers at the back can't see.

man, 69
London

BUS JOURNEY

Bank, St Pauls
and Elephant and Castle
Turnham Green
and Peckham Rye.

Bang your balls
on the elephant's arsehole
turn'em green
and peck'em ripe.

man, 68
London

PICCADILLY LINE

Is this Cockfosters?
No, it's mine.

man, 68
London

Where have you gone, Willy, Willy?
Up the town, Willy, Willy
Where's your money, Willy, Willy?
In my pocket, Willy, Willy.
Let me feel, Willy, Willy.
Feel your own, Willy, Willy.

boy, 9
Scotland

A man's occupation
is to stick his cockulation
in the woman's fertilisation
to make the next generation.

girl, 14
London

What's the time?
Half past nine,
hang your knickers
on the line.

When a copper
comes along,
take them off
and put them on.

man, 42
Middlesex

Sung

When Suzy was a baby,
a baby Suzy was,
she went ga ga
a ga-ga-ga
a ga ga ga ga ga-ga-ga.

When Suzy was a toddler,
a toddler Suzy was,
she went scribble, scribble
scribble-scribble-scribble
scribble scribble scribble-scribble-scribble.

When Suzy was a Junior,
a Junior Suzy was,
she went Miss, Miss,
I need to go a piss,
I don't know where the toilet is.

When Suzy was a Secondary,
a Secondary Suzy was,
she went ooh ah,
I've lost my bra,
I left my knickers in my boyfriend's car.

When Suzy was a mummy,
a mummy Suzy was,
she went sh sh sh-sh-sh
sh sh sh sh sh-sh-sh. (rocking baby)

When Suzy was a granny,
a granny Suzy was,
she went knit knit knit-knit-knit
knit knit knit knit knit-knit-knit.

When Suzy was a skeleton,
a skeleton Suzy was,
she went rattle rattle rattle-rattle-rattle
rattle rattle rattle-rattle-rattle.

When Suzy was a ghost,
a ghost Suzy was, she went oo oo oo-oo-oo
oo oo oo oo oo-oo-oo.

When Suzy was an angel,
an angel Suzy was.
she went amen amen amen
start again.

girl, 7
London

Sung

You ought to see Michael make water.
He makes such a beautiful stream.
It runs for a mile and a quarter,
And you can't see poor Michael for steam.

man, 68
London

Tune: Conga

In 1984
the monkeys had a war
they lost their guns
and used their bums
in 1984.

In 1986
the queen pulled down her nicks
she licked her bum
and said: 'Yum yum
it tastes like candy sticks.'

In 1987
the king went to heaven
he went so quick
he lost his dick
in 1987.

girl, 7
London

Down in sweet Texas where the cow shit lay thick,
I lay on the grass with my hands on my prick,
waiting for the girl that I love and adore,
Sweet Mary, oh my dairy, my girl for evermore.

boy, 11
London

Tune: An English Country Garden

What do you do
if you want to do a poo?
In an English Country Garden.

Pull down your pants
and suffocate the ants.
In an English Country Garden.

Then get some grass
and wipe it up your arse.
In an English Country Garden.

Then get a leaf
and wipe your underneath.
In an English Country Garden.

Then get a spade
and bury what you made.
In an English Country Garden.

That's what you do
If you want to do a poo,
In an English Country Garden.

girls, 7
London

Here I sit broken hearted
paid my penny
and only farted.

man, 42
Middlesex

My friend Billy's got a ten foot willy,
he showed it to the girl next door.
She thought it was a snake
so she hit it with a rake,
and now it's only four foot four.

woman, 38
Northern Ireland

I was walking down the lane,
when I felt a little pain,
diarrhoea
diarrhoea.

People think it's funny,
but it's really very runny,
diarrhoea
diarrhoea.

I sat down on a chair,
and it squirted everywhere,
diarrhoea
diarrhoea.

I sat down at school,
and it squirted on the wall,
diarrhoea
diarrhoea.

I went to the headmaster,
and it came out even faster,
diarrhoea
diarrhoea.

I went to the doctors,
but now I haven't got
diarrhoea
but the doctor's feeling queer
diarrhoea
diarrhoea.

girl, 7
London

Baked Beans – good for your heart,
the more you eat – the more you fart.
The more you fart, the better you feel,
so eat baked beans for every meal.

man, 42
Middlesex

Batman and Robin were in Batmobile,
Batman done a fart and paralysed the wheel.
The brakes couldn't take it
the engine fell apart,
all because of Batman and his supersonic fart.

boy, 11
London

Sung

The white cat piddled in the black cat's eye
and the black cat said 'Gor Blimey!
I wouldn't have piddled in the white cat's eye
if I knew she was behind me.'

woman 38,
Northern Ireland

Little bird flying high
drops his luggage from the sky.
Angry farmer wipes his eye
thanking god that cows don't fly.

man, 42
Middlesex

Oh shit! said the king
and his word was the law,
thirty thousand courtiers
straining on the floor.

man, 42
Middlesex

Dear Mr Johnson,
I am very sorry
but you will have to excuse Vicky for PE
she has diarrhoea.
It runs in the family.

girl, 13
London

Sung

In the German nick
where they hang you by the prick
and they pin dirty pictures on the walls
your mind goes blank
and you're dying for a wank
and the mice play ping pong with your balls.

boys, 12
London

'twas a dark and stormy night,
The lavatory was dim.
There came a crash
and then a splash.
Good god! she's fallen in.

girl, 13
London

Tune: Yellow Rose of Texas

There is a winding passage
that leads up to my heart,
and what comes down this passage
is commonly called a fart.
The fart is very useful
it sets the mind at ease.
It warms the bed on wintry nights
and disinfects the fleas.

man, 42
Middlesex

Creepy crawly custard
green snot pie,
all mashed up with a dead dog's eye.
Slugs and bogies spread on thick
all washed down
with a cup of cold sick.

girl, 13
London